SNAPSHOTS IN HISTORY

DRED SCOTT
v. SANDFORD

A Slave's Case for Freedom and Citizenship

by Sharon Cromwell

DRED SCOTT V. SANDFORD

A Slave's Case for Freedom and Citizenship

by Sharon Cromwell

Content Adviser: Steve Remy, Ph.D., Associate Professor of History, Brooklyn College, City University of New York

Reading Adviser: Katie Van Sluys, Ph.D., School of Education, DePaul University

Compass Point Books ✦ Minneapolis, Minnesota

DRED SCOTT V. SANDFORD

⊕ COMPASS POINT BOOKS

151 Good Counsel Drive
P.O. Box 669
Mankato, MN 56002-0669

Copyright © 2009 by Compass Point Books
All rights reserved. No part of this book may be reproduced
without written permission from the publisher. The publisher takes
no responsibility for the use of any of the materials or methods
described in this book, nor for the products thereof.
Printed in the United States of America.

 This book was manufactured with paper containing
at least 10 percent post-consumer waste.

For Compass Point Books
Robert McConnell, XNR Productions, Inc., Catherine Neitge,
Ashlee Suker, LuAnn Ascheman-Adams, and Nick Healy

Produced by White-Thomson Publishing Ltd.
For White-Thomson Publishing
Stephen White-Thomson, Susan Crean, Amy Sparks,
Tinstar Design Ltd., Steve Remy, Peggy Bresnick Kendler,
and Timothy Griffin

Library of Congress Cataloging-in-Publication Data
Cromwell, Sharon, 1947-
  Dred Scott v. Sandford : A Slave's Case for Freedom and Citizenship
  / by Sharon Cromwell.
      p. cm.—(Snapshots in History)
  Includes bibliographical references and index.
  ISBN 978-0-7565-4098-2 (library binding)
1. Scott, Dred, 1809-1858—Trials, litigation, etc.—Juvenile
literature. 2. Sanford, John F.A., 1806- or 7-1857—Trials, litigation,
etc.—Juvenile literature.
3. Slavery—Law and legislation—United States—History—19th
century—Juvenile literature. I. Title.
  KF228.S27C76 2009
  342.7308'7—dc22   2008038922

Visit Compass Point Books on the Internet at
www.compasspointbooks.com
or e-mail your request to
custserv@compasspointbooks.com

LESLIE'S ILLUSTRATED NEWSPAPER

Entered according to Act of Congress, in the year 1857, by FRANK LESLIE, in the Clerk's Office of the District Court for the Southern District of New York. (Copyrighted June 22, 1857.)

No. 82.—VOL. IV.]   NEW YORK, SATURDAY, JUNE 27, 1857.   [PRICE 6 CENTS.

TO TOURISTS AND TRAVELLERS.

We shall be happy to receive personal narratives, of land or sea, including adventures and incidents, from every person who pleases to correspond with our paper.

We take this opportunity of returning our thanks to our numerous artistic correspondents throughout the country, for the many sketches we are constantly receiving from them of the news of the day. We trust they will spare no pains to furnish us with drawings of events as they may occur. We would also remind them that it is necessary to send all sketches, if possible, by the earliest conveyance.

VISIT TO DRED SCOTT—HIS FAMILY—INCIDENTS OF HIS LIFE—DECISION OF THE SUPREME COURT.

Whilst standing in the Fair grounds at St. Louis, and engaged in conversation with a prominent citizen of that enterprising city, he suddenly asked us if we would not like to be introduced to Dred Scott. Upon expressing a desire to be thus honored, the gentleman called to an old negro who was standing near by, and our wish was gratified. Dred made a rude obeisance to our recognition, and seemed to enjoy the notice we expended upon him. We found him on examination to be a pure-blooded African, perhaps fifty years of age, with a shrewd, intelligent, good-natured face, of rather light frame, being not more than five feet six inches high. After some general remarks we expressed a wish to get his portrait (we had made

ELIZA AND LIZZIE, CHILDREN OF DRED SCOTT.

efforts before, through correspondents, and failed), and asked him if he would not go to Fitzgibbon's gallery and

have it taken. The gentleman present explained to Dred that it was proper he should have his likeness in the "great illustrated paper of the country," overruled his many objections, which seemed to grow out of a superstitious feeling, and he promised to be at the gallery the next day. This appointment Dred did not keep. Determined not to be foiled, we sought an interview with Mr. Crane, Dred's lawyer, who promptly gave us a letter of introduction, explaining to Dred that it was to his advantage to have his picture taken for our paper, and also directions where we could find his domicile. We found the place with difficulty, the streets in Dred's neighborhood being more clearly defined in the plan of the city than on the mother earth; we finally reached a wooden house, however, protected by a balcony that answered the description. Approaching the door, we saw a smart, tidy-looking negress, perhaps thirty years of age, who, with two female assistants, was busy ironing. To our question, "Is this where Dred Scott lives?" we received, rather hesitatingly, the answer, "Yes." Upon our asking if he was home, she said,

"What white man dats dat wanter fne," was don't white men 'fraid o' der own business, and let de nigger 'lone! forne of dese days I'll send the nigger—but me a fuck.

DRED SCOTT. PHOTOGRAPHED BY FITZGIBBON, OF ST. LOUIS.   HIS WIFE, HARRIET. PHOTOGRAPHED BY FITZGIBBON, OF ST. LOUIS.

CONTENTS

A Fateful Decision

On March 6, 1857, the nine members of the U.S. Supreme Court filed into a cramped, barely lighted courtroom in the nation's Capitol in Washington, D.C. Chief Justice Roger Taney—in his 80th year—slowly led the procession.

On this chilly but sunny day, the highest court in the land was meeting to rule on a case involving a man and his family who lived in St. Louis, Missouri. That man's name was Dred Scott, and he was a slave. The outcome of his case would hasten the Civil War and play a part in bringing freedom and civil rights to all African-Americans.

Dred Scott was suing the man he believed to be his owner, John Sanford, for freedom for himself and his family. The case was called

Dred Scott, a slave, spent 10 years seeking freedom for himself and his family before his case was heard by the Supreme Court.

Dred Scott v. Sandford because a court clerk had misspelled Sanford's name.

Scott's lawyer, Montgomery Blair, had first begun to argue the case before the Supreme Court more than a year before. Since then a national debate over slavery had taken hold of the country. Quarrels between the supporters and opponents of the expansion of slavery had grown more spirited. People on both sides were greatly interested in learning what the court would do. Important questions about slavery would be decided by the ruling.

Scott was not in the courtroom. He had continued working in St. Louis throughout the yearlong appeal. Because Scott was a slave, he had no legal rights. His battle for freedom for himself, his wife, Harriet, and their two daughters, Eliza and Lizzie,

THE NEW PRESIDENT'S POSITION ON SLAVERY

Slavery was on the minds of many Americans on March 6, 1857. Two days earlier the swearing in of President James Buchanan had captured the nation's attention. Americans wondered what the new president would do about the deep and worsening divide between those who wanted to limit slavery and those who supported its expansion. As a Northerner Buchanan might join other Northerners in opposing the spread of slavery. But as a Democrat he needed support from Southerners in his party who wanted slavery allowed in the newer territories. In the end Buchanan showed he was a "doughface"—a Northerner who supported slavery.

had lasted more than a decade before this fateful day. Scott felt that he and his family should be freed because his owners had brought him to a territory where slavery was illegal before bringing him back into a slave state again. The decision of the Supreme Court would do more than determine

President James Buchanan was sworn in on March 4, 1857.

the fate of Scott and his family. It would affect the future of slavery in the United States.

Newspaper reporters and spectators were packed in the courtroom. The *New York Tribune* said of the court's cramped chambers: "What a potato hole of a place this is! The old men ought to be got up above ground where they can breathe fresh air and see real daylight once in a while!"

THE SUPREME COURT

In 1857, of the nine justices serving on the Supreme Court, four were from the North and five were from the South. Most of the justices supported slavery and did not back slaves in their bids for freedom. The justices included John McLean, a Northerner, who had served on the Supreme Court the longest of all the justices. James M. Wayne had served the second longest term. The youngest member of the court was John A. Campbell.

The journalists were ready to report on the decision in *Dred Scott v. Sandford*, ready to bring news of the decision to the rest of the country.

Chief Justice Taney began to read a summary of the court's decision. The audience grew still, eager not to miss a word. Taney had a low voice that was difficult for the spectators to hear. He softly read the decision:

> *It is the opinion of the court ... that neither Dred Scott himself, nor any of his family, were made free by being carried into this territory; even if they had been carried there by the owner, with the intention of becoming a permanent resident.*

Taney's words destroyed the idea that slaves were "once free, forever free." This idea came from an earlier case in which the Missouri Supreme Court had ruled that a slave was free because her owner had once taken her into free territory. Taney went on to say that black men were "beings of an inferior order ... so far inferior, that they had no rights which the white man was bound to respect."

The Supreme Court announced its decision in the old Supreme Court Chamber in the U.S. Capitol.

13

Chief Justice Roger Taney was born in 1777 to a wealthy, slave-owning family.

After Taney finished reading, all the other justices presented their positions. The reading of their opinions continued into the next day. In the end, by a vote of 7-2, the court denied Dred Scott and his family their freedom. The majority of the justices ruled that Dred Scott was not a citizen.

WINNY V. WHITESIDES

Dred Scott's lawsuit was not the first of its kind. In a similar case in 1824 called *Winny v. Whitesides*, a slave named Winny won her freedom from her owner, Phoebe Whitesides, when the Missouri Supreme Court ruled in her favor. Whitesides had taken Winny from Kentucky, a slave state, to the Indiana Territory, where slavery was banned. Later the Whitesideses settled in Missouri Territory, and there Winny sued to attain her freedom.

The opinion of the court's majority was that a slave owner who took a slave into a free territory "and by the length of his residence there indicates an intention of making that place his residence & that of his slave gives a jury reason to believe that his slave has become a free man." The legal term "once free, forever free" came from the *Winny* case and similar court rulings. In other cases, courts in Missouri, Kentucky, and Louisiana had often freed slaves who had lived in free states or territories.

Therefore, under the U.S. Constitution, he had no right to sue for his freedom. On the other hand, the two dissenters, Benjamin Curtis and John McLean, held that blacks were eligible for United States citizenship. They also argued that Scott had become free in Illinois and had remained so after his return to Missouri. But Curtis and McLean were outvoted. The court decided that no one descended from Africans could be a U.S. citizen. The ruling applied to free African-Americans in the North as well as those enslaved in the South. In addition, the court said, the Constitution prohibited Congress from banning slavery in federal territories—large pieces of land that were part of the United States but not yet states.

Earlier legal cases did not sway the Supreme Court's decision in the *Dred Scott* case. Instead the high court found that the idea of "once free, forever free" was invalid. The Supreme Court often makes

Justice John McLean of Ohio had a history of making antislavery decisions in his judgments.

decisions that overrule decisions of lower courts, and that is what happened in the case of Dred Scott. One job of the Supreme Court is to make the final ruling in a case—a ruling no other court in the nation can overturn.

Taney and many supporters of the decision believed it would help settle the heated controversy over slavery. Instead the decision fanned its flames, and Americans soon realized that the slavery debate was far from over. Antislavery Northerners vowed to fight even harder against what many of them called an evil institution. Southerners, on the other hand, felt confident in the future of slavery. Yet the *Dred Scott* decision helped to bring about the Civil War, which began four years later. ◣

A Slave Culture

Chapter

2

Slavery in North America began in the British colony of Jamestown, Virginia, in 1619—more than 200 years before the *Dred Scott* decision. In the early days of slavery, the number of African slaves was relatively small. Early colonists were more likely to use indentured workers than slaves. Colonists who needed workers would pay for the ship passage of their workers—usually white Europeans, but also some Africans—who then worked for the colonists to pay them back for the journey. It cost twice as much to buy a strong, healthy slave as it did to pay for an indentured worker's passage.

In the mid-1600s, life for the working poor in Great Britain improved. Fewer indentured white workers left for the American colonies. Since Britain was a major source of indentured workers,

Slaves were held at a dock after leaving a Dutch man-of-war.

this reduced the number of people available to work in North America. Still in need of workers, more colonists decided to buy slaves to work their land. Slavery was most common in the South, where the owners of large farms called plantations needed many workers. All the British colonies in North America, however, eventually made slavery legal. During the transatlantic slave trade of the 1700s, 11 million to 12 million enslaved Africans came to the Americas. They were shipped in brutal conditions, with barely enough food and water to keep them alive.

Once sold to their North American owners, enslaved people were often treated as if they were less than human. They were forced to work from before dawn to after sundown. Most of them planted, tended, and picked crops in brutal heat. A few worked as cooks, butlers, or maids. Their food consisted mainly of corn and pork. They had no freedom at all. They could not even move from

A SLAVE'S PUNISHMENT

Colonial laws called for the harsh punishment of slaves. The Virginia Negro Code of 1699 outlined the punishment that slaves would receive for various crimes. It stated:

For the first offence of hog stealing commited by a Negro or slave he shall be carried before a justice of the peace of the county where the act was commited before whome being convicted of the said offence by one evidence or by his owne confession he shall … receive on his bare back thirty nine lashes well laid on, and for the second offence such Negro or slave upon conviction before a court of record shall stand two hours in the pillory and have both his eares nailed thereto and at the expiration of the said two hours have his eares cutt off close by the nailes.

place to place except with their owner's permission. Punishment of slaves was harsh, even in the early days of slavery. Some states passed laws that called for the whipping of slaves, or worse, for relatively minor "crimes" such as learning to read or write.

An engraving from the 1850s showed some ways slaves were punished.

21

Over the years slaves developed their own culture, which differed by place but often combined African and American ways of life. They developed their own approaches to marriage and family matters, even though slaves were limited by laws and family members might be sold off

Though illegal, weddings of slaves took place in secret.

without warning. Historians estimate that most slaves were sold at least once in their lives. Once sold, they almost certainly would never be reunited with their family members.

As part of their culture, slaves made their own musical instruments and invented dances. African music influenced them. Most slaves were not allowed to learn to read or write, but they created and told folktales to their children. They practiced medicine, using the roots of plants to treat their illnesses. In the slave quarters on the plantations, they took care of each other as much as possible.

Religious practices among slaves varied from plantation to plantation, but in general slaves believed in one supreme being and in the difference between good and evil. African rituals were also practiced by slaves, often in secret after owners forbade them.

In 1787, after the American Revolution, representatives from the colonies gathered to create a constitution. In a compromise between Northern and Southern states, the U.S. Constitution recognized the institution of slavery. In what is known as the Enumeration Clause, slaves were referred to as "other persons." They were counted as three-fifths of a whole person when tallying a state's population. In Article 1, Section 9, Congress was forbidden from prohibiting the "importation" of slaves until 1808. This meant the slave trade would continue, but it put a question mark over its future. Congress passed a law that outlawed the importation of slaves starting on January 1, 1808. But states still relied on slaves born in the United States.

Two young children watched a man and a young girl operate a cotton gin.

As tobacco and rice farming slowed in the late 1700s, the Southern economy relied less on slave labor. But the cotton gin, invented in 1793, changed that. The cotton gin made it much easier to process cotton for the market. However, more slaves were needed in the South to grow and process the larger cotton crop on which planters depended. So the invention of the cotton gin, which saved labor, led to an increase in slavery.

The economy of the North was not based on farming and did not rely on slaves. In addition many Northerners believed that treating people like property was wrong. As a result Northern states passed laws banning slavery. A divide developed between Northerners and Southerners because of their differences over slavery.

Before long the abolitionist movement rose in the North. It had its roots in the Protestant branch of Christianity in New England and the beliefs of liberalism, which favored freedom for all people. ◣

Scott's Early Years

Although no one knows his birthdate for sure, Dred Scott most likely was born between 1795 and 1800 in Southampton County, Virginia. Records show that his parents were owned by the family of Peter Blow. The babies of slaves became the property of their families' owners as soon as they were born. So when Dred was born, he too became the property of the Blow family.

Sickness in Dred's youth may have slowed his growth. Records show he was short as a man. He may have played with Thomas Vaughan, the first child of Peter Blow and his wife, Elizabeth. Thomas was born in 1804. At night the young Dred may have slept on the floor in the room of the Blows' younger twin boys, Richard and William. That way he could have taken care of them if they awoke. Thomas, Richard, and

Slaves performed all kinds of tasks on Southern plantations.

William all died before they reached adulthood. In 1814, Elizabeth gave birth to Peter, who was named for his father, and another boy, Henry, was born in 1817. In all the Blows had 11 children. By this time Dred Scott had likely reached his late teens or early 20s—too old to care for the Blows' children—and he might have toiled in the plantation fields. The poor soil did not yield enough cotton for the Blow family to live well. So Peter Blow looked for an opportunity to move his family to a new place with more fertile land.

During the 1800s thousands of slaves worked on cotton plantations operating cotton gins.

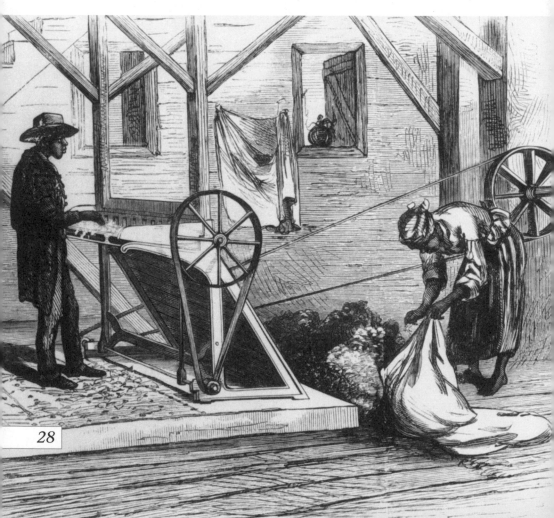

In 1818, Blow took Scott and his other slaves to a cotton plantation near Huntsville, Alabama. But again Blow had little success as a planter. In 1819, the national economy weakened. The price of cotton—the plantation's main crop—slipped from 25 cents a pound to 12 cents. This turn of events meant the Blow family had to move again. Blow had to sell his land for $5,000 to pay back money he had borrowed.

Dred Scott moved from place to place with the Blow family whenever Peter Blow wanted to live somewhere new. As Blow moved around in search of better fortune, the national divide over slavery deepened. In 1819, Missouri asked to join the Union. A fiery debate raged in Congress over whether to admit Missouri as a free state or a slave state. The opposing sides passionately hammered out the Missouri Compromise, which Congress passed in 1820.

Under the compromise, Maine joined the Union as a free state, and Missouri joined as a slave state. The compromise also banned slavery in all federal territories north and west of Missouri. Northerners saw the compromise as an important and basic part of U.S. law. They believed it would always keep slavery out of the western territories. On the other hand, many Southerners disliked the compromise because they thought it favored the North. Some of them believed it went against the U.S. Constitution.

The Missouri Compromise of 1820 only temporarily dealt with the issue of slavery in new territory.

In 1821, Scott moved again, this time to the busy town of Florence, Alabama. There Blow operated what became a thriving inn. Scott took care of guests' horses rather than serving as a field slave. Peter Blow decided in 1830 to again pull up roots, and he moved his family and slaves to the larger city of St. Louis, where slavery was legal. He believed St. Louis offered more chances for him to become rich. At this time the city had a population of 6,000. It was known as the gateway to the West—a label it still holds today.

In St. Louis Blow operated a boardinghouse called the Jefferson Hotel. His slaves, including Dred Scott, cleaned, cooked, and did other work in the hotel. But when the business did not bring in enough money, Blow hired out some of his slaves, including Scott, for cash. Because he needed money badly, Blow planned to sell Scott, along with some other male slaves.

Blow's wife, Elizabeth, died at the age of 46 in July 1831. Later that year their daughter Charlotte married Joseph Charless Jr. Blow's expenses for the funeral and the wedding made his money problems even worse. In 1832, Blow died after a short illness. Records do not show what was happening to the Blow family at that time or how that affected Scott's life.

It seems that Dred Scott was sold to Dr. John Emerson of St. Louis sometime before the end of 1833. It is not clear whether Peter Blow had sold Scott or Blow's daughter Elizabeth had sold him after her father's death.

Scott, in his early 30s, had always lived with the Blow family. Now he had a new owner who was close to his own age. How well he got along with Emerson is not known, because no records about their relationship exist. However, there is a story that Scott soon fled from Emerson and hid in a swamp—a sign of Scott's unhappiness with his new life. According to the story, he either returned on his own or was brought back to Emerson.

In 1833, Emerson joined the Army as a doctor and took Scott with him to Fort Armstrong in western Illinois. They arrived on December 1.

Slavery had been illegal in Illinois since 1787. When it became a state in 1818, its constitution banned slavery. But because no one was enforcing

the law, Scott still worked as a slave for Emerson while he lived at Fort Armstrong. Scott stayed there with Emerson until May 1836.

Fort Armstrong was on Rock Island, near where the Rock River and Mississippi River meet. When it rained the old fort's rotting buildings—

The riverfront in St. Louis was busy when Scott lived there in the early 1830s.

33

Fort Armstrong was built in 1816 and 1817 on Rock Island, Illinois, to protect what was then the frontier of the United States.

homes of officers and enlisted men—leaked. The small hospital room at the fort was so dirty that Emerson had the hospital moved into tents. The doctor's letters from the fort mention the dread of cholera, a disease that sickened and killed many men stationed there. The lives of Scott and

MANNING DEL.

W. WURTHACH. SC

the other slaves at the fort must have been more difficult than those of the soldiers. Emerson was especially unhappy at Fort Armstrong because the miserable conditions there made his health problems worse.

In 1836, the U.S. War Department decided to close Fort Armstrong. Emerson already had asked for a transfer. Scott traveled with Emerson by steamboat to Fort Snelling, a post located on land that was then part of the Wisconsin Territory but today is in St. Paul, Minnesota. By this time Scott had lived in Virginia, Alabama, Missouri, and Illinois. He most likely had no idea what to expect at his next home, which was farther north than he ever had lived or even traveled.

WHY WASN'T SCOTT FREED IN ILLINOIS?

In the early 1800s it was not unusual for U.S. Army officers to keep slaves, even in free states or territories. The U.S. government paid for food and clothing for the slaves in these situations. Even though slavery was banned in free states and territories, historians believe that most of the white population in Illinois opposed black equality. They would not have felt compelled to fight for Scott's freedom. Had Scott been able to read, he might have learned about the law in Illinois. But he could neither read nor write. Most likely, Scott did not even know at that time that he was living in a free state.

The Missouri Compromise meant that slavery was illegal in the Wisconsin Territory. However, as in Illinois, Scott might not have known he was living in a place where slavery was against the law. He and Emerson were in a frontier area, and no officials there enforced the law against Army officers such as Emerson who illegally kept slaves.

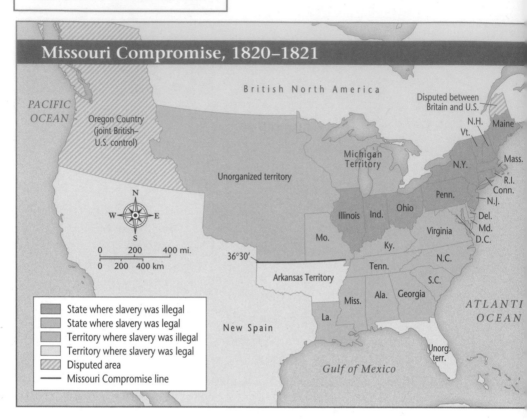

Missouri Compromise, 1820–1821

British North America

PACIFIC
OCEAN

Oregon Country
(joint British–
U.S. control)

Disputed between
Britain and U.S.

N.H.
Vt.
Maine

Unorganized territory

Michigan
Territory

N.Y.

Mass.
R.I.
Conn.
N.J.

Penn.

Illinois   Ind.   Ohio

Del.
Md.
D.C.

Mo.

Virginia

N

W   E

S

0   200   400 mi.

0   200   400 km

36°30'

Ky.

Tenn.

N.C.

Arkansas Territory

S.C.

Miss.   Ala.   Georgia

ATLANTIC
OCEAN

New Spain

La.

Unorg.
terr.

Gulf of Mexico

State where slavery was illegal
State where slavery was legal
Territory where slavery was illegal
Territory where slavery was legal
Disputed area
Missouri Compromise line

The Missouri Compromise line divided free states and territories from slave states and territories.

However, in the 1830s, there had been lawsuits in which slaves in similar situations had won their freedom. One such case was *Rachel v. Walker*. Rachel was first owned by T.B.W. Stockton, an Army officer. She had lived with him and his family at Fort Snelling. Later, when Rachel was owned by William Walker and lived in St. Louis, she sued for her freedom. She said she was no longer a slave because she had lived in the free Wisconsin Territory.

A court in St. Louis ruled that Rachel had no right to liberty. It said that, as an Army officer, Stockton could not pick his home. The court reasoned that because he had not chosen to take her to a free territory, she was still a slave. Rachel took her case to the Missouri Supreme Court in 1836. That court overruled the lower court and said Rachel was free. The court said a military officer lost his right to own a slave if he took the slave to a free territory, as Stockton had done. ◣

Scott's Travels

Chapter

4

During his two-year stay at Fort Snelling, Dred Scott married Harriet Robinson, a slave owned by Major Lawrence Taliaferro. Taliaferro was an agent who acted on behalf of the U.S. government in its dealings with Native Americans. He also was a justice of the peace, a low-level judge. Marriage of slaves was illegal throughout the country, but Taliaferro performed a civil marriage ceremony for the couple. Taliaferro either gave or sold Robinson to Scott's owner so she could live with her husband. The Scotts' marriage lasted until Dred Scott died, more than 20 years later.

Emerson thought the cold, snowy winters at Fort Snelling made him ill, so he again asked for a transfer. His request was approved, and in October 1837 he traveled to Jefferson Barracks

Little is known about the life of Harriet Robinson before she met and married Dred Scott at Fort Snelling.

in St. Louis. Emerson went down the Mississippi River by canoe at first because the upper part of the river was frozen and steamboats could not travel there. Later he continued by steamboat to St. Louis. But the canoe travel meant that Emerson could not take the Scotts with him. Instead he left them at Fort Snelling and hired them out to other officers.

According to the laws then, passing through a free state with an owner did not entitle a slave to freedom. But the fact that Emerson had rented the Scotts for money at Fort Snelling changed things. Based on Emerson's actions, all Northern state supreme courts and even some Southern judges would have supported Scott's claim to liberty—had he made such a claim then.

Emerson, possibly because of his poor health, never stayed at any of his posts for long. In November 1837 he was sent to Fort Jesup in western Louisiana, where he married Eliza Irene Sanford, who was known as Irene Sanford.

CIVIL MARRIAGE

A civil marriage is a marriage performed by a legal official instead of a religious official. The civil marriage of the Scotts was unusual. One reason slaves could not marry legally was that legal marriage between slaves might hinder an owner who wanted to sell the husband or wife. Opponents of slave marriage also argued that a civil marriage is a contract. Slaves could not enter into contracts in any state. Slaves in a legal marriage also might demand other rights, such as the right of wives and husbands not to give evidence against each other in criminal court cases. Under U.S. law, slave partners could be forced to give evidence against each other.

Officers at Fort Jesup, in Louisiana, lived in a two-story building.

In the spring of 1838, Emerson told Dred and Harriet Scott to come to Fort Jesup. They traveled to Louisiana, a slave state. The Scotts journeyed about 1,200 miles (1,920 kilometers) alone, down the Mississippi River. They went through towns in Iowa and Illinois where they might have escaped and found freedom. Or they might have left the boat in St. Louis and hidden among the city's free black population. Why they did not do so—maybe they feared being caught and separated—is unknown.

In October 1838 the Emersons and the Scotts returned to Fort Snelling because Emerson had requested another transfer. On their trip up the Mississippi, Harriet gave birth to the Scotts' first child, a girl. The birth happened in free territory, with the free state of Illinois and Wisconsin Territory on one side of the river, and the free territory of Iowa on the other. The Scotts named their daughter Eliza, after Eliza Irene Sanford Emerson. The Scotts later had a second daughter, Lizzie, and two sons who died when they were infants.

Two years later Emerson requested another transfer and was sent to a post in Seminole Indian country in Florida. The U.S. government had been fighting a war with the Seminoles, so Emerson went there alone—leaving his wife and the Scotts near St. Louis. Irene Emerson and the Scott family lived with Irene's father, Alexander Sanford, on his plantation. Dred and Harriet Scott were both hired out to other families during this time.

Emerson remained in Florida for more than two years. But he again complained about poor health and asked for another transfer. The Army—probably because of Emerson's repeated transfer requests—gave him an honorable discharge in August 1842.

Emerson returned to St. Louis, where he was reunited with his wife. By then Dred Scott had probably made contact with some of the then adult children of Peter and Elizabeth Blow, including Taylor Blow, who worked in a large business. The Blow children had prospered in the city, with several marriages into successful families. If Dred Scott had sought his freedom, the Blow family would have had enough money to help him. Much later, when he finally tried to escape slavery, they did help him.

Emerson was unhappy in St. Louis, where he had trouble finding patients for his medical practice. He asked for a new Army job. However,

The Second Seminole War between the United States and Native Americans took place from 1835 to 1842 in Florida.

before hearing from the Army, Emerson moved with his wife to Davenport, Iowa. He worked as a doctor and in real estate. Emerson most likely had left the Scotts in St. Louis, where they once again worked for other people to earn money for him.

In November 1842 a baby girl was born to the Emersons in Davenport. A year later Emerson died at 40 years of age. The official cause of his death

43

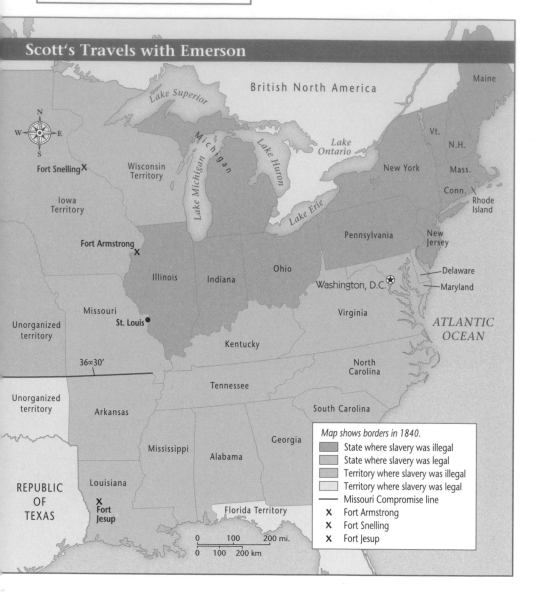

Scott's Travels with Emerson

British North America

Maine

Lake Superior

Michigan

Lake Huron

Lake Ontario

Vt.

N.H.

Fort Snelling ✕

Wisconsin Territory

Lake Michigan

New York

Mass.

Conn.

Iowa Territory

Rhode Island

Fort Armstrong ✕

Illinois

Indiana

Ohio

Lake Erie

Pennsylvania

New Jersey

Washington, D.C. ✪

Delaware

Maryland

Missouri

St. Louis ●

Virginia

ATLANTIC OCEAN

Unorganized territory

Kentucky

36∞30'

North Carolina

Tennessee

Unorganized territory

Arkansas

South Carolina

Map shows borders in 1840.

  State where slavery was illegal
  State where slavery was legal
  Territory where slavery was illegal
  Territory where slavery was legal
—— Missouri Compromise line
✕ Fort Armstrong
✕ Fort Snelling
✕ Fort Jesup

Mississippi

Alabama

Georgia

REPUBLIC OF TEXAS

Louisiana

✕ Fort Jesup

Florida Territory

0   100   200 mi.

0   100 200 km

Dred Scott lived at forts in Illinois, Wisconsin Territory, Iowa Territory, and Louisiana.

was tuberculosis, an infectious disease then known as consumption. In his will Emerson left his property to his wife. The will mentioned land and furniture as being Emerson's possessions. It said nothing about his slaves or their future.

For three years after her husband's death, Irene Emerson rented out the Scott family in St. Louis, as her husband had done. Dred Scott worked for Irene Emerson's brother-in-law, Army Captain Henry Bainbridge. For a time Scott worked at Jefferson Barracks, near St. Louis. Records do not show where Harriet and Eliza Scott lived then.

Scott went with Bainbridge to Fort Jesup, Louisiana—where he had previously stayed with Emerson—in 1844. There are indications Scott went to Texas with Bainbridge in 1845 and stayed with him in Corpus Christi, Texas, until February 1846.

Harriet Scott gave birth to the Scotts' second daughter, Lizzie, in 1846. Soon after that Dred Scott, who had returned to St. Louis, was hired out to work for Samuel Russell, the owner of a grocery. About that time Scott tried to buy his and his family's freedom from Irene Emerson, offering her $300 as a down payment. She turned down his offer.

Scott Claims to Be Free

Chapter

5

On April 6, 1846, Dred and Harriet Scott filed lawsuits for their freedom at the St. Louis County Courthouse. The Scotts claimed their freedom as well as the liberty of their two daughters. The suits were *Dred Scott v. Irene Emerson* and *Harriet Scott v. Irene Emerson*. Dred Scott's suit charged that Irene Emerson had "beat, bruised and ill-treated him" and then held him as a prisoner for 12 hours. He said he was a "free person" who was being held as a slave and asked for $10 in payment of damages. Harriet Scott's suit echoed her husband's.

Why the Scotts sued for freedom in Missouri, a slave state, instead of in the free state of Illinois is not clear. Possibly Emerson had said he would free Scott, but he did not carry out that promise in his will. Then Irene Emerson turned down

The old St. Louis County Courthouse, located in the heart of downtown St. Louis, was later turned into a museum.

Scott's offer to buy his own and his family's liberty. After her refusal, Scott may have thought his only choice was to sue her.

Why Irene Emerson turned down Scott's offer is not known either. At the time of his lawsuit, Irene Emerson was living with her father, Alexander Sanford, on his plantation. Sanford's pro-slavery beliefs most likely influenced Irene Emerson's actions following Scott's claim to freedom.

Dred Scott signed his lawsuit with an X.

It is not clear how Scott learned to ask the court to free him. Perhaps someone in the Blow family explained how to sue for liberty. Some sources point to another possibility. In the 1840s, Harriet Scott became a member of the Second African Baptist Church in St. Louis. The Reverend John R. Anderson, pastor of the church, had been born into slavery. As an adult he had bought his liberty and worked for an antislavery editor in Illinois. From Anderson or another church member, Harriet Scott may have found out that her family had a good chance to win freedom in court.

Francis Murdoch, the Scotts' first attorney, opposed slavery. Murdoch filed legal papers in which Dred Scott claimed he should be freed because John Emerson had transported him into Illinois and the Wisconsin Territory, places where slavery was illegal.

Murdoch had been the city attorney in Alton, Illinois, when Elijah Lovejoy—an abolitionist who wrote antislavery pamphlets—was killed there by a mob. Mob violence led to the deaths of several other people as well as the destruction of property. As the city's lawyer, Murdoch brought to trial those who committed crimes.

One result of the Lovejoy murder was that many people who opposed slavery left Alton, and Murdoch was one of them. He moved to St. Louis in 1841. It is possible he met the Scott family through the pastor of the church in St. Louis that was attended by Harriet Scott. The pastor once worked as Lovejoy's typesetter in Alton, and he was in Alton the night Lovejoy was killed. However, no record of a connection between Murdoch and Anderson exists. Murdoch's first known connection with Dred Scott is the lawyer's name on the legal papers filed by the Scotts against Irene Emerson. In 1847, Murdoch left St. Louis and moved to California.

When Scott's lawyer moved away soon after the trial began, Scott needed a new lawyer. Charlotte Blow Charless probably asked her brother-in-law, Charles Drake, to step in and help Scott. It is unknown whether Drake ever represented Scott in court, but he did help to prepare the case. In June 1847, Drake left St. Louis for a time. So again Scott was left without an attorney.

Scott's third lawyer was Samuel Mansfield Bay, a former Missouri attorney general. There is no record of why Bay took charge of the case. However, a connection between Bay and the Blow family may have been the reason. Bay was the lawyer for the Bank of Missouri. Joseph Charless Jr., the husband of Charlotte Blow Charless, had close ties to the bank, and Joseph Charless might have asked Bay to take over Scott's suit.

Scott's legal situation looked promising as the trial approached. The judge for his case was Alexander Hamilton, who in previous cases had shown sympathy toward slaves' claims for freedom. The Missouri Supreme Court had ruled in *Rachel v. Walker* that Rachel was free. No court decisions in Missouri since that time had changed the doctrine of "once free, forever free." When slaves were taken to a free state or territory, they

Charles Drake, who later became a senator, had increasingly strong antislavery feelings in the buildup to the Civil War.

were freed. Returning to the slave state of Missouri did not change that. One historian wrote:

> *Anyone familiar with Missouri law could have told the Scotts that they had a strong case. Again and again, the highest court of the state had ruled that a master who took his slave to reside in a state or territory where slavery was prohibited thereby emancipated [freed] him.*

At the trial Bay used witnesses to prove that Scott had lived on free soil with John Emerson in Illinois and the Wisconsin Territory. A problem arose, however, in proving that his widow, Irene Emerson, owned the Scotts. A witness who had hired the Scotts to work for him said he had paid Irene Emerson's father, not her, for their work. Henry Blow testified that his father, Peter Blow, had sold Scott to John Emerson, not Irene Emerson. While everyone knew that Irene Emerson owned the Scotts, the court ruled that her ownership could not be proven. The court decided against the Scotts on June 30, 1847. Dred Scott had lost his suit for freedom on a technicality.

HELP FROM THE BLOWS

Taylor Blow, a son of Peter Blow, was likely about 12 years old when Scott was sold to Dr. John Emerson. However Taylor Blow and Scott were linked later in their lives. The Blow family and their in-laws—an important family in St. Louis—aided Scott in 1846, when he first sued for freedom, and they went on helping him financially. Taylor Blow also gave Scott money and other support during the decade in which Scott's case made its way through the courts. It is not known why Blow helped Scott, but the help continued until Scott died.

The following day Bay, on behalf of the Scotts, asked for a new trial. Because of delays in the Missouri court system, Judge Hamilton did not decide to allow a retrial until December 2, 1847. At the same time, Irene Emerson's attorneys tried to legally prevent a new trial. Irene Emerson could not keep the Scotts in custody during their lawsuits because they claimed to be free. But because they were slaves, she had them held by

Slaves often worked while their white owners relaxed.

53

An illustration of Eliza and Lizzie Scott appeared on the front page of Frank Leslie's Illustrated Newspaper *on June 27, 1857.*

the sheriff of St. Louis County, who hired them out. Emerson had told him to keep the money they earned until the court made a decision. The sheriff held the Scotts in custody for almost 10 years, until after the U.S. Supreme Court ruled on their lawsuit in 1857.

C. Edmund LaBeaume, a lawyer, and Peter Ethelrod Blow, Taylor Blow's brother, helped Dred and Harriet Scott by giving them work at various times. During this time, Harriet Scott sent their children, Eliza and Lizzie, to stay with friends at a secret location. Why she felt the need to do this is not clear.

Attorney Alexander P. Field next took the Scotts' case. In April 1848 a hearing based on Irene Emerson's appeal opened. The court ruled against her. New trial dates were set for February 1849, then May 1849, but a citywide fire and cholera outbreak in St. Louis caused delays.

The second trial finally began on January 12, 1850, with Judge Alexander Hamilton again presiding. This time the Scotts' legal argument that Irene Emerson was their owner convinced the jury. The court's ruling made Dred Scott and his family free. The family's battle for permanent freedom, however, was far from finished. 🔺

Dred Scott: Free or a Slave?

Chapter

6

Dred Scott's case went through a number of complicated twists and turns. Irene Emerson refused to give up her claim on him. In March 1850 a motion was filed to appeal the case to the Missouri Supreme Court. That court put off its decision until 1852. Also in 1852, the lawyers on both sides of the *Dred Scott* case agreed that from then on appeals would be based on Dred's case alone, and that court decisions would also apply to Harriet Scott.

Until 1850 the *Dred Scott* case had attracted little attention outside Missouri. But as the case dragged through the courts, the controversy over slavery grew more heated. As the United States acquired more territory, most Southerners wanted to extend slavery into the West. In

An illustrated front page appeared in the antislavery newspaper Emancipator. *It told of how "native-born American" slaves were cruelly treated.*

EMANCIPATOR—*EXTRA.*

NEW-YORK, SEPTEMBER 2, 1839.

American Anti-Slavery Almanac for 1840.

The seven cuts following, are selected from thirteen, which may be found in the Anti-Slavery Almanac for 1840. They represent well-authenticated facts, and illustrate in various ways, the cruelties daily inflicted upon three millions of native born Americans, by their fellow-countrymen! A brief explanation follows each cut.

The peculiar "Domestic Institutions of our Southern brethren."

Selling a Mother from her Child.

Mothers with young Children at work in the field.

A Woman chained to a Girl, and a Man in irons at work in the field.

"They can't take care of themselves"; explained in an interesting article.

Hunting Slaves with dogs and guns. A Slave drowned by the dogs.

Servility of the Northern States in arresting and returning fugitive Slaves.

57

accordance with the Missouri Compromise, Northerners generally supported a ban on slavery in western territories.

In 1846, the United States went to war with Mexico. With victory, the United States gained more western lands, including the territory of California,

The Mexican War lasted from 1846 to 1848.

which applied for admission to the union as a free state in 1850. In response to the Mexican War, Congress passed five laws known as the Compromise of 1850. The laws were intended to settle territorial and slavery disputes.

California was admitted to the union as a free state, which pleased Northerners. The sale of slaves was banned in Washington, D.C., also pleasing Northerners. Southerners, on the other hand, welcomed a tougher fugitive slave law, which took away captured slaves' right to a jury trial and their right to testify on their own behalf. Southerners also favored provisions that left open to slavery lands won from Mexico other than California. The Compromise of 1850 reflected the growing divide between the North and South more than a decade before the Civil War began.

In the following years, opposition to slavery deepened among Northerners, particularly those who considered it an immoral institution. Southerners, even many who did not own slaves, resented the Northerners' attitude toward life in their region. Most people in slaveholding states had no sympathy for slaves who sued for their freedom.

WHO OWNED DRED SCOTT?

Irene Emerson claimed that she had given ownership of Dred Scott to her brother, John Sanford. Sanford's lawyers again and again stated that Sanford owned Scott. Sanford also testified that the Scotts were his "lawful property." But there is no bill of sale or other record to prove Sanford's claim. And Sanford—who died two months after the Supreme Court decision—did not state in his will that he owned the Scotts.

Public opinion in Missouri affected the outcome of Dred Scott's second lawsuit. Because their state was bordered by free territory on three sides, Missourians were particularly aware of the national debate over slavery. The antislavery movement was a minority in Missouri, but it worried slave owners nonetheless.

In time Scott's case went to the Missouri Supreme Court. On March 22, 1852, Judge William Scott announced the court's 2-to-1 decision. Judge Scott finished by saying:

> *The introduction of slavery amongst us was, in the providence of God, ... a [way] of placing that unhappy race [Africans] within the pale of civilized nations.*

The court ruled that Scott had always been a slave and remained a slave. It said Harriet Scott and their daughters, Eliza and Lizzie, were also slaves. The Scott family had lost its freedom. A historian wrote of the court's decision:

> *For the first time, politics was injected into the case, not by the parties, but by the judges of the Missouri Supreme Court.*

Meanwhile Irene Emerson had moved to Massachusetts and remarried. Marrying Calvin Chaffee, a Republican congressman, she was now known as Irene Chaffee. Her brother, John Sanford, had moved to New York, leaving Dred Scott in St. Louis.

In November 1853 Dred Scott filed a lawsuit against John Sanford in the federal district court in St. Louis. In the suit Scott claimed damages of $9,000 against Sanford for assaulting and wrongfully imprisoning him, Harriet, and their two children. Sanford may have seen himself as Scott's

Because of a lack of courtroom space in the county courthouse, Scott's federal trial was held in a private building.

owner because he had been given the power to manage Emerson's estate after the doctor died. However Irene Emerson had controlled Dred and Harriet Scott's lives for years, and that may be why the Scotts first sued her for their freedom.

Roswell M. Field replaced David Hall and Alexander Field as Scott's lawyer. Roswell Field, who was not related to Alexander Field, planned to take the case to the U.S. Supreme Court. He wanted

Roswell M. Field, who brought Dred Scott's case to the Supreme Court, was born in Vermont and held strong antislavery beliefs.

an answer to a huge question that applied to the whole country: Were slaves "once free, forever free"? If slaves had lived in a free state or territory, were they then permanently free?

In the spring of 1854, the federal judge presiding in the *Dred Scott v. Sandford* case, Robert Wells, sided with the Missouri Supreme Court. Scott, he ruled, had always been a slave and would remain one. Scott's lawyer, Roswell Field, asked for a new trial, but Judge Wells refused. The next move was to take Scott's case to the U.S. Supreme Court in Washington, D.C. ◣

The Final Decision

The Blow family had already provided money to pay Scott's legal costs, but a Supreme Court trial would be expensive. To help raise money, Charles LaBeaume, who had earlier aided the Scotts by giving them work, wrote and sold a 12-page pamphlet about Dred Scott's case. LaBeaume wrote as if he were Scott:

> *I have no money to pay anybody at Washington to speak for me ... Will nobody speak for me at Washington, even without hope of other reward than the blessings of a poor black man and his family?*

Months passed, and almost no one responded with help. Finally in December 1854, a respected Washington lawyer, Montgomery Blair, agreed to take Dred Scott's case without a fee. Blair

Montgomery Blair came from a powerful family in Washington, D.C. His brother was a U.S. senator.

then found an opponent of slavery to pay the court costs. John Sanford hired two powerful lawyers, Henry S. Geyer and Reverdy Johnson, to represent him. Geyer was a U.S. senator from Missouri. Johnson had been the U.S. attorney general—the nation's top lawyer—under President Zachary Taylor.

The *Dred Scott* case was filed on December 30, 1854. But because of a crowded court calendar, the case was delayed for more than a year. Dred and Harriet Scott continued working—hired out by Sanford—in St. Louis.

MONTGOMERY BLAIR TAKES THE CASE

Montgomery Blair's family had political power in both Washington and St. Louis. They belonged to the upper class of the South. But unlike most people in their social class, they opposed the expansion of slavery. A skilled antislavery lawyer such as Blair was needed to represent Dred Scott, whose story was now well known to newspaper readers across the nation. Gamaliel Bailey, editor of the antislavery journal *National Era*, said he would pay Scott's court costs.

On February 11, 1856, Dred Scott's case was heard by the Supreme Court. The chief justice of the United States, the court's leading member, was Roger B. Taney of Maryland. In arguing Scott's case before the court, Montgomery Blair made three basic points: First, when slaves were taken into a free state or territory by their owners, those slaves were considered free according to common law. Second, the "once free, forever free" idea supported Scott's claim to freedom, even though he had eventually been returned to Missouri, a slave state. Last, Scott was an American citizen because he had lived in the United States his entire life.

Sanford's lawyers flatly rejected Blair's three points. They argued that Congress did not have the power or right to limit slavery. Scott, they

Reverdy Johnson, one of John Sanford's lawyers, was a former U.S. senator from Maryland.

67

said, had always been a slave and was still a slave. As a slave, they said, he was not a U.S. citizen and therefore had no right to claim his freedom in the courts.

On March 6, 1857, the Supreme Court handed down its ruling in *Scott v. Sandford*. Two justices voted in favor of Scott. Seven justices voted against him. The majority declared that Scott was a

The U.S. Supreme Court now meets in an impressive building in Washington — not in the cramped quarters where the Dred Scott decision was handed down.

U.S. SUPREME COURT IN 1857

Four justices on the court at the time of the *Dred Scott* decision were Northerners, and five were Southerners. Seven justices had been chosen for the court by Southern presidents who owned slaves. Northern presidents had appointed Benjamin R. Curtis of Massachusetts and Peter Daniel of Virginia. The region that the justices, or the presidents who appointed them, came from might have affected the justices' thinking in the *Dred Scott* case.

The Supreme Court was composed of the following justices:

Justice	State	Appointed By (state of birth in parentheses)
John Campbell	Alabama	Franklin Pierce (New Hampshire) in 1853
John Catron	Tennessee	Andrew Jackson (South Carolina) in 1836
Benjamin Curtis* **	Massachusetts	Millard Fillmore (New York) in 1851
Peter Daniel	Virginia	Martin Van Buren (New York) in 1841
Robert Grier	Pennsylvania	James K. Polk (North Carolina) in 1846
John McLean*	Ohio	Andrew Jackson in 1830
Samuel Nelson	New York	John Tyler (Virginia) in 1845
Roger Taney***	Maryland	Andrew Jackson in 1836
James Moore Wayne	Georgia	Andrew Jackson in 1835

* Dissenters who voted in favor of Dred Scott
** Brother of Dred Scott's attorney, George T. Curtis
*** Chief Justice

slave. Harriet, Eliza, and Lizzie Scott were also considered slaves. Eleven years of court hearings, delays, and rulings had ended with the Scott family still enslaved.

The court said Scott was still bound by the laws of Missouri, even though he had lived in the free state of Illinois and in the free Wisconsin

Chief Justice Taney read the summary of the court's decision.

Territory. It also rejected Scott's claim that he was free because he had lived in a territory made free by the Missouri Compromise. In fact six of the nine justices went beyond what the case required and declared the Missouri Compromise unconstitutional. In addition the court decided that Congress had no power to decide where slavery was allowed.

One of the two justices who disagreed with the decision, John McLean, argued that Dred Scott was a United States citizen. He and the other dissenter, Benjamin Curtis, argued that blacks had taken part in American politics even before the American Revolution. Blacks, they pointed out, had voted as citizens.

In his opinion, Curtis argued:

> [By the time of the American Revolution] ... all free native-born inhabitants of the States of New Hampshire, Massachusetts, New York, New Jersey, and North Carolina, though descended from African slaves, were not only citizens of those States, but such of them as had the other necessary qualifications possessed the franchise of electors, on equal terms with other citizens.

While the Supreme Court's ruling pleased Southerners, it enraged Northerners. Newspapers throughout the nation reacted to the court's ruling with strong statements. In the *Mercury* of

Charleston, South Carolina, editor Robert Barnwell Rhett, who supported slavery, wrote that the decision meant "slavery is guaranteed by the constitutional compact." A newspaper in Augusta, Georgia, offered the opinion that Southerners' ideas about slavery had become the law of the nation.

CURTIS RESIGNS

Supreme Court Justice Benjamin Curtis resigned from the court in disgust over the ruling in the *Dred Scott* case. He is the only Supreme Court justice ever to resign over a matter of principle. Curtis was born in Massachusetts in 1809. He attended Harvard Law School and was appointed to the Supreme Court in 1851.

On the other hand, Taney's opinion deeply angered abolitionists, who opposed slavery and supported the rights of African-Americans. Abolitionist Horace Greeley—editor of the *New York Tribune*—called the court's decision "atrocious," "wicked," and "abominable."

A fiery newspaper headline in the *New York Independent* read: "Wickedness of the Decision in the Supreme Court against the African Race." The *Independent* also published an editorial headlined "The Decision of the Supreme Court is the Moral Assassination of a Race and Cannot be Obeyed." The *Whig and Courier*, a newspaper in Bangor, Maine, labeled the *Dred Scott* decision a "monstrous doctrine" that took away from Maine's black citizens "the ordinary justice which the meanest [lowest] individual of any other race of foreign people may obtain [receive] among us."

What Frederick Douglass—an African-American speaker, editor, and later U.S. ambassador—said and wrote about the *Dred Scott* decision reveals a point of view that few people of the time could have shared. By 1850 Douglass had become the most famous African-American in the United States.

Frederick Douglass advised President Abraham Lincoln during the Civil War.

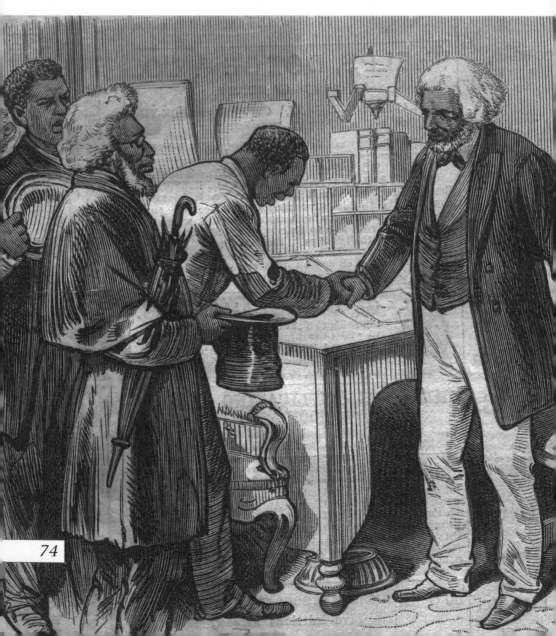

Born a slave in Maryland in 1818, Douglass escaped to the North. He edited a newspaper, the *North Star*, in Rochester, New York. In a speech after the *Dred Scott* decision, Douglass said, "The more the question [of slavery] has been settled, the more it has needed settling." In the Supreme Court decision, Douglass saw "one necessary link in the chain of events preparatory to the downfall and complete overthrow of the whole slave system." Even though he thought the ruling was a bad one, he believed it would finally lead to the end of slavery.

Ending the speech, Douglass said:

All I ask of the American people is, that they live up to the Constitution, adopt its principles, imbibe [take in] its spirit and enforce its provisions. When this is done, the wounds of my bleeding people will be healed, the chain will no longer rust on their ankles, their backs will no longer be torn by the bloody lash, and liberty, the glorious birthright of our common humanity, will become the inheritance of all the inhabitants of this highly favored country.

Since the Dred Scott Case

After the Supreme Court's ruling, Dred Scott's life did not change right away. He went on working as a janitor in law offices in St. Louis. Even though John Sanford had triumphed in the Supreme Court, he did not benefit. He died in a mental institution on May 5, 1857, just two months after the court decision.

After the court ruled, Irene Chaffee's husband, U.S. Representative Calvin Chaffee, claimed she still owned Dred Scott. He said she had never given or sold him to her brother. Chaffee told a newspaper: "I regard Slavery as a sin against God and a crime against man." Irene Chaffee decided to transfer ownership of the Scott family to Taylor Blow in Missouri, so Blow could free them.

Frank Leslie's Illustrated Newspaper *featured a front-page story on the Supreme Court's* Dred Scott *decision in 1857. The story included pictures of Dred and Harriet Scott and their children, Eliza and Lizzie.*

FRANK LESLIE'S
ILLUSTRATED
NEWSPAPER

Entered according to Act of Congress, in the year 1857, by FRANK LESLIE, in the Clerk's Office of the District Court for the Southern District of New York. (Copyrighted June 22, 1857.)

No. 82.—VOL. IV.]   **NEW YORK, SATURDAY, JUNE 27, 1857.**   [PRICE 6 CENTS.

TO TOURISTS AND TRAVELLERS.

WE shall be happy to receive personal narratives, of land or sea, including adventures and incidents, from every person who pleases to correspond with our paper.

We take this opportunity of returning our thanks to our numerous artistic correspondents throughout the country, for the many sketches we are constantly receiving from them of the news of the day. We trust they will spare no pains to furnish us with drawings of events as they may occur. We would also remind them that it is necessary to send all sketches, if possible, by the earliest conveyance.

VISIT TO DRED SCOTT—HIS FAMILY—INCIDENTS OF HIS LIFE—DECISION OF THE SUPREME COURT.

WHILE standing in the Fair grounds at St. Louis, and engaged in conversation with a prominent citizen of that enterprising city, he suddenly asked us if we would not like to be introduced to Dred Scott. Upon expressing a desire to be thus honored, the gentleman called to an old negro who was standing near by, and our wish was gratified. Dred made a rude obeisance to our recognition, and seemed to enjoy the notice we expended upon him. We found him on examination to be a pure-blooded African, perhaps fifty years of age, with a shrewd, intelligent, good-natured face, of rather light frame, being not more than five feet six inches high. After some general efforts before, though correspondents, and failed, and remarks we expressed a wish to get his portrait (we had made asked him if he would not go to Fitzgibbon's gallery and

ELIZA AND LIZZIE, CHILDREN OF DRED SCOTT.

have it taken. The gentleman present explained to Dred that it was proper he should have his likeness in the "great illustrated paper of the country," overruled his many objections, which seemed to grow out of a superstitious feeling, and he promised to be at the gallery the next day. This appointment Dred did not keep. Determined not to be foiled, we sought an interview with Mr. Crane, Dred's lawyer, who promptly gave us a letter of introduction, explaining to Dred that it was to his advantage to have his picture taken to be engraved for our paper, and also directions where we could find his domicile. We found the place with difficulty, the streets in Dred's neighborhood being more clearly defined in the plan of the city than on the mother earth; we finally reached a wooden house, however, protected by a balcony that answered the description. Approaching the door, we saw a smart, tidy-looking negress, perhaps thirty years of age, who, with two female assistants, was busy ironing. To our question, "Is this where Dred Scott lives?" we received, rather hesitatingly, the answer, "Yes." Upon our asking if he was home, she said,

"What white man arter dad nigger fur?—why don't white men 'tend to his own business, and let dis nigger 'lone? Shan' of dem days dey is sure business, and let dis nigger 'lone? Shan' steal dat nigger—dat are a fact."

DRED SCOTT. PHOTOGRAPHED BY FITZGIBBON, OF ST. LOUIS.   HIS WIFE, HARRIET. PHOTOGRAPHED BY FITZGIBBON, OF ST. LOUIS.

On May 26, 1857, Dred and Harriet Scott went before Judge Alexander Hamilton, who had been the judge in their case 10 years earlier. Taylor Blow signed the legal papers giving up his ownership of them. At long last the Scotts were permanently free.

The *Dred Scott* decision influenced important events in politics, including the new antislavery Republican Party. In 1858, Republican Abraham Lincoln ran for election to the U.S. Senate from Illinois. His opponent was Democratic U.S. Senator Stephen A. Douglas. The two faced off in what are known as the Lincoln-Douglas debates. Douglas argued for popular sovereignty—allowing slavery in a territory if the residents voted for it. Lincoln opposed the idea. In a famous speech on June 16, 1858, at the state Republican convention in Springfield, Lincoln used the *Dred Scott* decision as an example of how the supporters of slavery were gaining power:

> *"A house divided against itself cannot stand." I believe this government cannot endure, permanently half slave and half free. I do not expect the Union to be dissolved— I do not expect the house to fall—but I do expect it will cease to be divided. It will become all one thing, or all the other. Either the opponents of slavery, will [stop] the further spread of it, and place it where the public mind shall rest in the belief that it is in course of ultimate extinction*

> *[end]; or its advocates will push it forward, till it shall become alike lawful in all the States, old as well as new—North as well as South.*

Lincoln argued during the Lincoln-Douglas debates that the *Dred Scott* decision had moved the United States toward becoming a nation in which slavery would be legal in the North as well as the South.

Stephen A. Douglas, wearing a black suit and white shirt, stood behind Abraham Lincoln during a debate.

Douglas responded to the speech by claiming that Lincoln supported:

> *Boldly and clearly a war of sections [regions], a war of the North against the South, of the free states against the slave states—a war of extermination—to be continued relentlessly until the one or the other shall be subdued and all the states shall either become free or become slave.*

In the election that fall Douglas was re-elected to the Senate. However, the previously little-known Lincoln had gained fame because of the debates. He again ran against Douglas in 1860—this time for the presidency. Lincoln won that election.

Living in St. Louis, the Scotts went on working as always, but because they were no longer considered slaves, they received pay. Dred Scott carried guests' luggage at the Barnum Hotel, and his wife did laundry. Newspapers reported that Eliza and Lizzie ran away from home but had come back by 1858. At last the Scott family was reunited.

On September 17, 1858, Dred Scott died, probably from tuberculosis, an illness he had battled for some time. He had been free for just over a year.

AN OFFER REFUSED

Dred and Harriet Scott were asked to travel around the country and tell the emotional tale of their journey from slavery to freedom. The tour would have earned them $1,000—a lot of money in the 1850s. However they turned down the offer. They apparently had no wish to relive their experiences.

Most of the newspaper stories about Scott's death were short. However some editors wrote about the impact that the *Dred Scott* decision would have. "In ages yet to come," said the *New York Herald*, "Dred Scott and the decision which bears his name will be familiar words ... [to] the student of political history."

Scott was buried in an unmarked grave in a cemetery that later was closed as St. Louis grew. However, in 1867, Taylor Blow had Scott's remains buried again—in the Blow family plot at Calvary Cemetery in St. Louis. Scott's grave received a granite headstone given by a granddaughter of Taylor Blow in 1957. That ceremony was part of a centennial marking the 100th anniversary of the *Dred Scott* decision. On one side of the tombstone, these words were carved:

DRED SCOTT
BORN ABOUT 1799
DIED SEPT. 17, 1858
FREED FROM SLAVERY BY
HIS FRIEND, TAYLOR BLOW

On the other side of his tombstone is this inscription:

DRED SCOTT
SUBJECT OF THE DECISION OF
THE SUPREME COURT OF THE
UNITED STATES IN 1857 WHICH
DENIED CITIZENSHIP TO THE
NEGRO, VOIDED THE MISSOURI
COMPROMISE ACT, BECAME
ONE OF THE EVENTS THAT
RESULTED IN THE CIVIL WAR.

It is not clear what happened to Dred Scott's family after his death. Eliza is thought to have died in 1863. Harriet died June 17, 1876. Her grave was recently found in a cemetery in Hillsdale, Missouri. Lizzie is thought to have married Henry Madison of St. Louis. She died in 1884. In 1957, several of the Madisons' descendants attended the centennial ceremony.

Legal historians have called the *Dred Scott* decision a terrible mistake. It deepened the split between Northerners and Southerners over slavery, and it made civil war more likely. The

Supreme Court's ruling angered Northern voters. In 1860, it was one reason many Northerners voted for antislavery candidate Abraham Lincoln for president of the United States.

South Carolina left the union a month after Lincoln was elected. Soon six more Southern states united with South Carolina as the Confederate States of America. Their goal was to safeguard the rights of slave owners. The Civil War between the North and South began in 1861. It grew into a conflict over slavery as well as different ways of life in the North and South.

The Battle of Gettysburg was one of the bloodiest clashes of the Civil War.

83

When the North won the contest in 1865, Lincoln had already freed many slaves with the 1863 Emancipation Proclamation.

After the war amendments to the Constitution made important changes in the rights of African-Americans. In December 1865 the 13th Amendment to the Constitution abolished slavery. Ratified in 1868, the 14th Amendment stated that everyone born or naturalized in the United States, including blacks, shared equal benefits of citizenship. The 15th Amendment, ratified in 1870, guaranteed the right of citizens (that is, male citizens) to vote regardless of race or whether they had been slaves. From then on, the civil rights that Dred Scott and

A popular magazine ran an image of a gathering held in 1866 to celebrate the Civil Rights Act. The act said all persons born in the United States were citizens, without regard to race, color, or previous condition.

other Americans had battled for were guaranteed by the Constitution for African-American men.

By the end of the 1860s black men had new legal rights. Like white men, they could vote, serve on juries, enter into legal contracts, file lawsuits, own and inherit property, and use public railroads, inns, and theaters. Yet states could still restrict voting by taxing voters and requiring that they own property or be able to read. Beginning in the 1870s the U.S. Supreme Court, in decisions such as *Plessy v. Ferguson*, overturned some federal laws protecting the rights of black Americans. The court's rulings further eroded their voting rights and kept them from serving on juries.

In the middle of the 20th century, Supreme Court decisions took a new turn when the justices began to rule in support of the civil rights of African-Americans. The court finally rejected former Chief Justice Taney's view that descendants of Africans belonged to an inferior race. One important case—*Brown v. Board of Education*—in 1954 ended the separation of blacks and whites in schools.

Since that time the Supreme Court's landmark *Dred Scott* decision has been remembered time and again. The court's denial of Scott's freedom inspired other African-Americans and their supporters to fight for civil rights well into the 20th century. Dred Scott's quest so many years ago continues to shine as an example of what one person can do in the pursuit of liberty. ◣

Timeline

1619

The first enslaved Africans to be brought to North America arrive in Jamestown, Virginia.

1795 to 1800

Dred Scott most likely is born during this time in Southampton County, Virginia, becoming the property of the Peter Blow family.

1818

Scott and Peter Blow's other slaves are taken to a cotton plantation near Huntsville, Alabama, where Scott works as a field hand.

1820

The Missouri Compromise bans slavery in territory north and west of Missouri.

1821

Scott moves to Florence, Alabama, where Blow operates a thriving inn.

1830

Scott moves to St. Louis, Missouri, to work at a boardinghouse Blow operates.

1832

Peter Blow dies after a short illness.

1833

Dred Scott is sold to Dr. John Emerson.

December 1, 1833

Scott and Emerson arrive at Fort Armstrong in Rock Island, Illinois. For the first time, Scott lives in a state where slavery is banned.

May 8, 1836

Scott, again traveling with Emerson, reaches Fort Snelling in the Wisconsin Territory.

1836 or 1837

Scott marries Harriet Robinson in a civil marriage ceremony performed by Major Lawrence Taliaferro, a government agent and justice of the peace.

October 20, 1837

Emerson leaves Fort Snelling for Jefferson Barracks in St. Louis, but hires the Scotts out to other officers at Fort Snelling.

February 6, 1838

Emerson marries Eliza Irene Sanford, known as Irene, in Louisiana.

April 1838

Dred and Harriett Scott journey from Fort Snelling to Fort Jesup, Louisiana, to join the Emersons.

October 21, 1838

The Scotts and Emersons arrive at Fort Snelling, where Emerson again had been sent by the Army.

May 29, 1840

Dred and Harriet Scott, with their daughter, Eliza, and the Emersons, leave Fort Snelling. Emerson goes on to a new assignment in Florida, leaving his wife, Irene, and the Scotts in St. Louis.

August 26, 1842

Emerson is discharged from the Army and returns to St. Louis, where he is reunited with his wife.

December 29, 1843

Emerson dies from tuberculosis while living in Davenport, Iowa.

1844 to 1846

Irene Emerson rents out the family slaves, including the Scotts, in St. Louis, as her husband had done.

1846

Harriet Scott gives birth to the Scotts' second daughter, Lizzie.

April 6, 1846

Dred and Harriet Scott file suit for their freedom at the St. Louis County Courthouse. They also claim the liberty of their two daughters.

June 30, 1847

The Scotts lose their suit against Irene Emerson on a technicality—no testimony in court proves they were owned by her. The Scotts' lawyer asks for a new trial.

February 1849

A new trial was supposed to begin at this time, but the case is delayed because of too many court cases.

May 1849

The trial was expected to start at this time, but the case is delayed because of a cholera outbreak in St. Louis.

1849 or 1850

Irene Emerson moves from St. Louis to Massachusetts, leaving behind the Scotts and her other slaves.

January 12, 1850

In a new trial, the Scotts' lawyers prove that Irene Emerson was their owner. The court rules that Dred Scott and his family are free.

March 8, 1850

Irene Emerson and her lawyers file an appeal with the Missouri Supreme Court. The court puts off its decision until 1852.

November 21, 1850

Irene Emerson marries Calvin Chaffee, a member of Congress.

Timeline

March 22, 1852

In a 2-1 ruling, the Missouri Supreme Court decides that Scott has always been a slave and remains a slave.

November 2, 1853

Dred Scott sues John Sanford, Irene Emerson Chafee's brother, for his freedom, filing the lawsuit in federal district court in Missouri.

May 15, 1854

The U.S. District Court rules that Dred and Harriet Scott and their daughters are slaves and the property of John Sanford.

December 30, 1854

The U.S. Supreme Court puts the *Dred Scott* case on its schedule.

March 6, 1857

Dred Scott and his family are denied their freedom by a 7–2 vote of the Supreme Court; the court decides that no one descended from Africans is a U.S. citizen.

May 26, 1857

The Scott family is freed by a judge in St. Louis after Taylor Blow, to whom they were transferred by Irene Chafee, gives up ownership of them.

September 17, 1858

Dred Scott dies, probably from tuberculosis.

April 1861

The Civil War begins.

January 1, 1863

The Emancipation Proclamation, issued by President Abraham Lincoln, frees all slaves in the rebellious South.

HISTORIC SITES

Old Courthouse
11 N. 4th St.
St. Louis, MO 63102
314/655-1700

The courthouse is part of the Jefferson National Expansion Memorial, which includes the St. Louis Arch.

U.S. Supreme Court
First Street and Maryland Avenue
Washington, D.C. 20543
202/479-3211

The Supreme Court is open for tours; it offers exhibits and educational programs.

LOOK FOR MORE BOOKS IN THIS SERIES

The Bataan Death March:
World War II Prisoners in the Pacific

1963 Birmingham Church Bombing:
The Ku Klux Klan's History of Terror

Tiananmen Square:
Massacre Crushes China's Democracy Movement

A complete list of **Snapshots in History** titles is available on our Web site: *www.compasspointbooks.com*

89

Glossary

abolitionist
person who supported the banning of slavery

civil rights
person's rights that are guaranteed by the U.S. Constitution

common law
unwritten law based on judges' decisions and custom

compromise
settlement in which each side gives up part of its demands and agrees to the final product

Constitution
legal document that describes the basic form of the U.S. government and the rights of citizens

custody
immediate charge and control of a suspect exercised by an authority

economy
the way a country produces, distributes, and uses its money, goods, natural resources, and services

inferior
lower in rank or status

man-of-war
armed sailing ship

naturalized
admitted to citizenship

technicality
small inconsistency, such as the wrong address, that is used as a reason to dismiss a lawsuit

territory
area that belongs to the United States but is not yet organized as a state

Source Notes

Chapter 1

Page 12, line 10: Department of Political Science. University of California, Berkeley. www.polisci.berkeley.edu/courses/coursepages/Spring2005/ps157/2005Lect19.pdf

Page 12, line 24: *Scott v. Sandford*, U.S. Supreme Court. 60 U.S. 393 (1857).

Page 13, line 2: *Winny v. Whitesides*, Missouri Supreme Court. 1 Mo. 472 (1824).

Page 13, line 6: *Scott v. Sandford.*

Page 15, sidebar lines 9 and 12: *Winny v. Whitesides.*

Chapter 2

Page 20, sidebar line 7: William Waller Hening. *Hening's Statutes at Large.* 22 Oct. 2008. www.vagenweb.org/hening/vol03-11.htm

Chapter 5

Page 46, line 7: *Scott v. Emerson,* St. Louis, Mo., circuit court. 6 April 1846.

Page 46, line 9: Ibid.

Page 52, line 3: Don E. Fehrenbacher. *The Dred Scott Case: Its Significance in American Law and Politics.* New York: Oxford University Press, p. 272.

Chapter 6

Page 59, sidebar line 8: Ibid.

Page 60, lines 12 and 21: *The Dred Scott Case: Its Significance in American Law and Politics,* p. 265.

Page 63, line 2: *Winny v. Whitesides.*

Chapter 7

Page 64, line 8: *Dred Scott: Person or Property?* p. 46.

Page 66, line 28: *Winny v. Whitesides.*

Page 72, line 17: U.S. Supreme Court Justice Benjamin Robbins Curtis, (dissenting), *Scott v. Sandford.*

Page 73, line 5: Robert Barnwell Rhett. "The Past and the Future." *Mercury* (Charleston, South Carolina), 17 March 1857.

Page 73, line 16: Horace Greeley. Editorial. *Tribune* (New York). 7 March 1857.

Page 73, line 19: "Wickedness of the Decision in the Supreme Court against the African Race." *Independent.* New York. 19 March 1857.

Page 73, line 22: "The Decision of the Supreme Court is the Moral Assassination of a Race and Cannot be Obeyed." *Independent.* (New York). Reprinted in *The Liberator,* Boston, Massachusetts. 3 April 1857.

Source Notes

Page 73, lines 26 and 27: *Whig and Courier*. (Bangor, Maine). 15 March 1857.

Page 75, lines 4 and 7 and 14: Frederick Douglass. Pamphlet based on *The Dred Scott Decision: Speech at New York, on the Occasion of the Anniversary of the American Abolition Society.* 11 May 1857.

Chapter 8
Page 76, line 12: *The Dred Scott Case: Its Significance in American Law and Politics*, p. 568.

Page 78, line 21: Ibid.

Page 80, line 3: Paul Finkelman. *Dred Scott v. Sandford: A Brief History with Documents*. New York: Bedford/St. Martins, 1997.

Page 81, lines 4 and 5: *New York Herald*. 22 Sept. 1858.

SELECT BIBLIOGRAPHY

Copeland, David A. *The Antebellum Era: Primary Documents on Events from 1820 to 1860*. Westport, Conn.: Greenwood Press, 2003.

Ehrlich, Walter. *They Have No Rights: Dred Scott's Struggle for Freedom*. Westport, Conn.: Greenwood Press, 1979.

Fehrenbacher, Don E. *The Dred Scott Case: Its Significance in American Law and Politics*. New York: Oxford University Press, 2001.

Finkelman, Paul. *Dred Scott v. Sandford: A Brief History With Documents*. Boston: Bedford/St. Martin's, 1997.

Ratner, Lorman A., and Dwight L. Teeter Jr. *Fanatics & Fire-Eaters: Newspapers and the Coming of the Civil War*. Chicago: University of Illinois Press, 2003.

FURTHER READING

McNeese, Tim. *Dred Scott v. Sandford: The Pursuit of Freedom*. New York: Chelsea House, 2007.

Moses, Sheila P. *I, Dred Scott: A Fictional Slave Narrative Based on the Life and Legal Precedent of Dred Scott*. New York: Margaret McElderry, 2005.

Naden, Corinne J., and Rose Blue. *Dred Scott: Person or Property?* New York: Benchmark Books, 2005.

Skog, Jason. *Dred Scott Decision*. Minneapolis: Compass Point Books, 2006.

Index

95

ABOUT THE AUTHOR

Sharon Cromwell lives with her husband and their son in Chester, Connecticut. She has written a number of nonfiction books and many newspaper articles for young readers. She also writes for a weekly newspaper. She loves to read, travel, and spend time with friends.

IMAGE CREDITS